CREATED BY CHRIS

WITH CAM[

GIFT of HEAVEN

PRODUCTS AVAILABLE
Choral Book 0-6330-1634-9 • Listening Cassette 0-6330-1635-7
Listening CD 0-6330-1636-5 • Accompaniment Cassette 0-6330-1637-3
Accompaniment CD 0-6330-1638-1 • Rehearsal Tracks 0-6330-1639-X
Orchestration 0-6330-1642-X • Cassette Promo Pak 0-6330-1643-8
CD Promo Pak 0-6330-1644-6 • Poster Pak 0-6330-1641-1
Bulletins 0-6330-1640-3

INSTRUMENTATION INCLUDES:
Flute1-2, Oboe, Clarinet 1-2, Trumpet 1, Trumpet 2-3, French Horn 1-2,
Trombone 1-2, Trombone 3/Tuba, Timpani, Percussion, Drums,
Rhythm (Piano, Bass, Guitar), Harp, Violin 1-2, Viola, Cello, String Bass

SUBSTITUTE/OPTIONAL PARTS:
Alto Sax 1-2 (for Horn 1-2); Tenor Sax (for Trombone 1-2);
Baritone TC (for Trombone 1-2); Clarinet 3 (for Viola); Bassoon;
Bass Clarinet; Keyboard String Reduction

G
GENEVOX

© Copyright 2001 GENEVOX. Nashville, TN 37234.
Possession of a CCLI license does not grant you permission to make copies of this piece of music.
For clarification about the rights CCLI does grant you, please call 1-800-234-2446.

Foreword

When I have the opportunity to work on choral collections or musicals, I am always on the lookout for great songs. When I was asked to arrange and orchestrate *Gift of Heaven*, I knew that the search would not be necessary since I would be working with Chris and Diane Machen. I consider them to be two of our finest communicators of the gospel through music. Their songs and their testimony have blessed my life numerous times in the last decade or so, and I value this opportunity to be a part of presenting their musical offering.

God bless you as you focus on every word of every song. I pray that as a singer, instrumentalist, or director, your life will be touched, once again, by the greatest story ever told.

Camp Kirkland
Jacksonville, Florida

Every year as the Christmas season approaches, we find ourselves getting caught up in the exciting, but sometimes overwhelming, activity of list-making and gift-buying that is such a part of our holiday celebration. Finding just the right gift for that special person is important, and is a tangible way of showing our love for them. But as thoughtful and expensive as these earthly gifts may be, they can never satisfy the greatest needs and desires of the human heart such as peace, hope, joy, love, and eternal life. These gifts can only be found wrapped up in One package—Jesus, the Greatest Gift of all, sent from the very heart of God. May your heart be renewed and full of joy this Christmas as you thank God for the Indescribable Gift He has given you—Jesus, the Gift of Heaven!

Chris and Diane Machen
Dallas, Texas

SEQUENCE

OVERTURE/PROCESSIONAL 5
includes
The First Nowell
Joy to the World! The Lord Is Come

GIFT OF HEAVEN (Opening) 9
includes
Gift of Heaven
For a Child Will Be Born

HOUSE OF BREAD (Underscore) 17
HOUSE OF BREAD 18

THE WAYS OF GOD (Underscore) 28
THE WAYS OF GOD 29

WHEN HOPE WAS BORN 43
with
O Holy Night!

REPEAT THE SOUNDING JOY 54
with
Joy to the World! The Lord Is Come

THEY CAME TO WORSHIP 66
with
Angels, from the Realms of Glory

WORTHY OF MY LORD 78
with
More Precious than Silver
O Come, All Ye Faithful

FROM THE CRADLE TO THE CROSS 87

GIFT OF HEAVEN (Finale) 100
includes
Gift of Heaven
For a Child Will Be Born
Repeat the Sounding Joy

Production Notes 117

Overture/Processional

includes
The First Nowell
Joy to the World! The Lord Is Come

Arranged by Camp Kirkland

© Copyright 2001 Van Ness Press, Inc. (ASCAP).
Nashville, TN 37234.

18
G♭maj7/A♭
D♭
mf
E♭m7
D♭2/F
D♭/F
21
G♭
A♭
G♭/B♭
A♭/C
D♭
A♭/C
24
B♭m
Fm
G♭
D♭/F
E♭m7
Fm7
G♭maj7
G♭maj7/A♭
A♭7
rit.
Faster ♩ = 114
2
B♭
27
29
A♭/B♭
31
E♭
A♭
E♭/B♭
B♭
E♭

33
A♭
B♭
E♭
B♭/E♭
E♭
36
E♭
B♭7/E♭
39
E♭/G
A♭
E♭/G
A♭
E♭/B♭
A♭
E♭/B♭
B♭7
E♭
3
41
F
C/B♭
F/A
B♭
F/C
C♯dim7
Dm
Dm/C
F/C
f
43
Gm7
C
D♭
E♭2
F
45
Gm7
F/A
B♭maj7
F/C
F/E♭
B♭2/D
B♭m(♯7)

F/C
47
C7
49
A/C♯
Dm
B♭
Gm7
F/C
C♯dim7
Dm
B♭
51
F/C
53
Gm/C
segue to "Gift of Heaven (Opening)"
Am/C
Gm/C
Am/C
Gm/C
Am/C
56
grad. rit.

Gift of Heaven (Opening)

includes
Gift of Heaven
For a Child Will Be Born

Words and Music by
CHRIS and DIANE MACHEN
Arranged by Camp Kirkland

(Continue rit.)

With power ♩ = 80

Je - sus, gift of heav - en, Je - sus,

pre - cious gift of love from the heart of God to the

© Copyright 2001 Van Ness Press, Inc. (ASCAP).
Nashville, TN 37234.

8
hearts of men,
Je - sus, gift of
G/B C G/B Am7 G/B
5
10
heav - en.
Dsus D G
Stronger
unis.
12
Je - sus, gift of heav - en, Je - sus,
unis.
A♭ B♭m7 Cm7 E♭/F A♭/E♭ D♭ A♭/C
Stronger

pre-cious gift— of love from the heart of God to the hearts of men,— Je-sus, gift of heav-

*FOR A CHILD WILL BE BORN**

*Words and Music by Chris and Diane Machen.
© Copyright 2001 Van Ness Press, Inc. (ASCAP). Nashville, TN 37234.

31
peo - ple who walk in dark - ness,
name shall be called Won - der - ful
Am7
G/B
D
Em
33
they shall see a great Light.
In the
Coun - se - lor, Might - y God.
Ev - er -
D/F♯
G
D
Em
C
G/B
35
unis.
land of shad - ows of death and night,
the
last - ing Fa - ther, the Prince of Peace,
the
unis.
Am7
G/B
D
Em

Light will shine. For a Child will be
Light will shine
come. For a Child will be
born, and a Son will be given.
For a Child will be born, given.

46
unis.
div.
For a Child will be born,
and a Son will be
For a Child will be born,
Bbm/Ab Ab Bbm/Ab Ab Db
Eb/Db Dbmaj7 Eb
49
1.
2.
given.
For a Child will be given.
Eb/Ab Ab Bbm/Ab Ab
52
The Light has come,
the Light has
Ab/C Db Eb

come, _____ the Light has come, _____

the Light has come, _____ He has

come. _____

House of Bread (Underscore)

Arranged by Camp Kirkla.

NARRATION: *(music starts)* For God so loved the world that He gave: He gave light to those in darkness; He gave hope to those without hope; He gave life and joy and love; He gave Jesus. In the mystery of His marvelous grace, God spoke through His prophets to a world in need of a Savior. A virgin would bear a Son conceived of the Holy Spirit; the Word would become flesh and dwell among us, and His name would be called Emmanuel, God with us. And in that same mysterious plan, God would choose one of the smallest, most out-of-the-way places for the Savior of the world to be born: Bethlehem, tiny Bethlehem. They called it the House of Bread—strangely appropriate, for from the House of Bread would come the Bread of Life, Jesus, who would give the gift of life to all.

House of Bread

Words and Music by
CHRIS and DIANE MACHEN
Arranged by Camp Kirkland

With energy ♩ = 100
"...strangely appropriate..."

A ti-ny stop a-long the road, a vil-lage dark and small, a most un-like-ly birth-place of Light and Life for all.

© Copyright 2001 Van Ness Press, Inc. (ASCAP).
Nashville, TN 37234.

O little town of Bethlehem, they call the House of Bread, from you will come the Gift of Life, just as the prophets

19
f
said.
From the
F
21
unis.
House of Bread will come the Bread of Life, and who-ev-er be-lieves in
unis.
B♭ C Dm C B♭ Gm7
f
24
div.
unis.
Him will live for-ev - er and ev - er, and nev-er
div.
unis.
A B♭ C Dm C B♭

hun-ger or thirst a - gain. From the gain, nev-er

hun-ger or thirst a - gain.

lit - tle town of Beth - le - hem you seem too small to

add LADIES **mf**
too small to be the
be

place where God would touch the world for all e - ter - ni -

e - ter - ni - ty. Yet,

ty.

all the world will know your name, this place called Beth - le -

hem. A

Child born in the House of Bread will change the hearts of men. From the House of Bread will come the Bread of Life, and who-ev-er be-lieves in

Him will live for-ev-er and ev-er, and nev-er hun-ger or thirst a-gain. From the gain, nev-er hun-ger or thirst a-gain. From the

63
unis.
House of Bread will come the Bread of Life, and who-ev-er be-lieves in
unis.
The House, the Bread of Life, who - ev - er be-
D♭ E♭ Fm E♭ D♭ B♭m7
ff
66
div.
Him will live for-ev - er and ev - er, and nev-er
div.
lieves in Him
C D♭ E♭ Fm E♭ D♭
69
1. 2.
hun-ger or thirst a - gain. From the gain, nev-er
B♭m7 E♭ Fm D♭

27

The Ways of God (Underscore)

Arranged by Camp Kirkland

NARRATION: *(music starts)* The appointed place was Bethlehem. The chosen parents were a young maiden named Mary and a poor carpenter named Joseph. They were engaged to be married when an angel came to them and turned their world upside-down. Mary was with child. "How can this be?" she asked the angel. And the angel replied, "With God, nothing shall be impossible." These were the words of hope that Mary and Joseph would embrace and believe. And as they followed God in His sovereign plan, surely the words of Isaiah the prophet also rang in their hearts, for Isaiah spoke the words of God, "As the heavens are higher than the earth, so are My ways higher than your ways." In the midst of the unbelievable, still Mary and Joseph believed.

The Ways of God

Words and Music by
CHRIS and DIANE MACHEN
Arranged by Camp Kirkland

my name, he said, "Mar-y, you're the one." Just a few days a-go my world for-ev-er changed; an an-gel said to me, "Your bride to be is car-ry-ing God's Son." I know my

SOLO (Joseph)

DUET (Joseph sings bottom note, at pitch)

31

life is in His hand, e-ven if I do not un-der-stand.

17 (1st time)
19 (2nd time)

The ways of God some-times are hard

CHOIR

The ways of God

— to com - pre-hend — what's im - pos - si - ble — for me is pos - si - ble — for Him. The ways of God —

Ooo —

The ways of God —

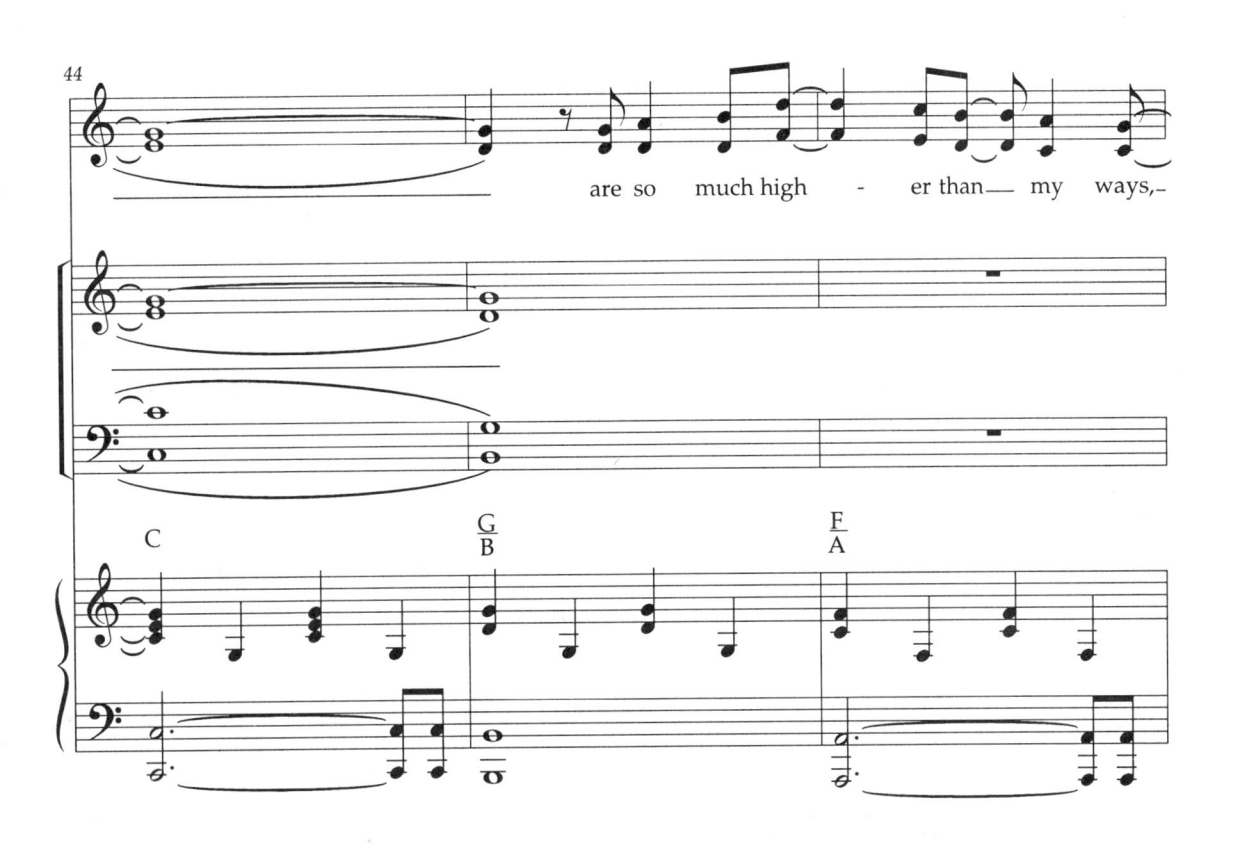

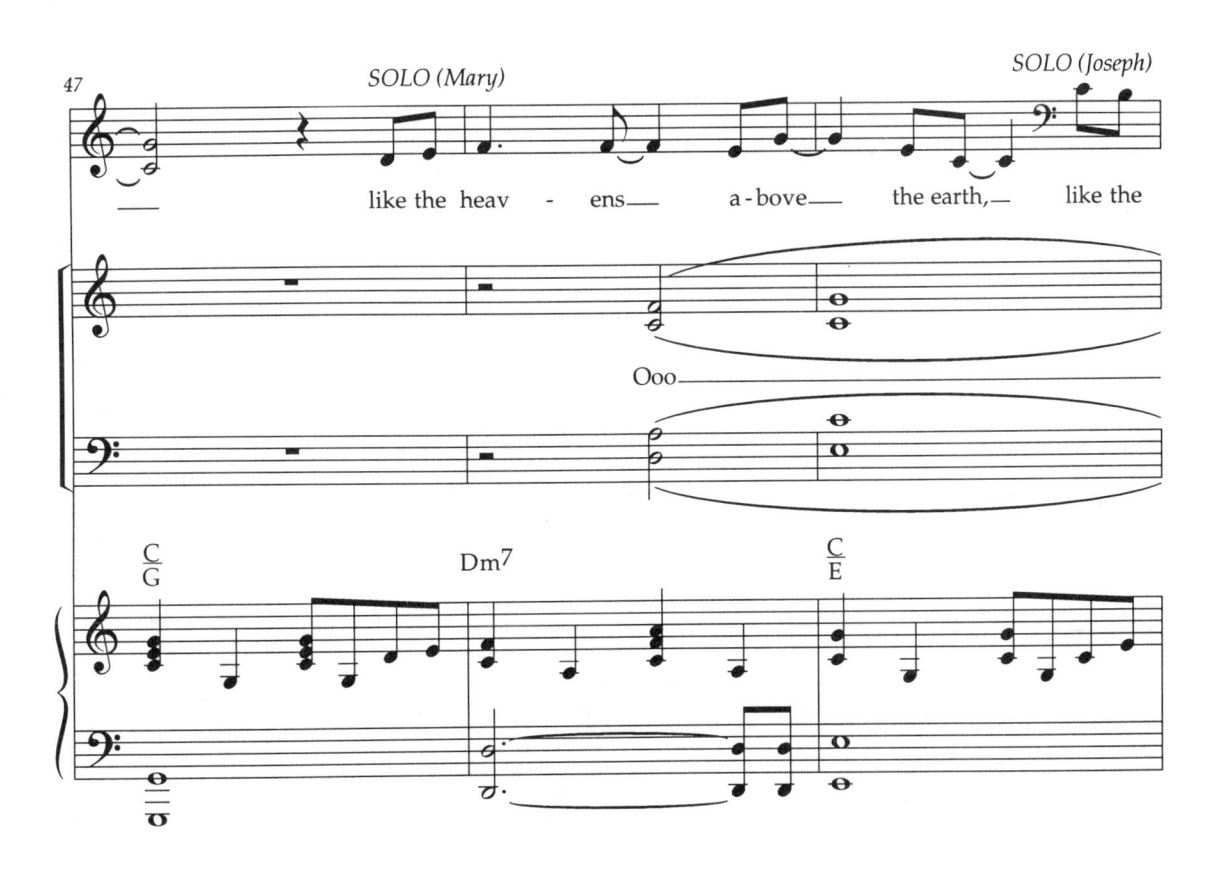

are so much high - er than my ways,

SOLO (Mary) like the heav - ens a-bove the earth, *SOLO (Joseph)* like the

Ooo

mir - a - cle of Je - sus' birth. Still I will trust

DUET

Still I will trust

F | G | Am | Dm7 | G/C | F/B♭

20 *(2nd time)*
DUET unison   2nd time to Coda ⊕

the ways of God.

2nd time to Coda ⊕
F/G | C2

18

SOLO (Joseph)
mp

Just a

few days from now, when the Child of God arrives, will I understand how this simple man can be a father to God's Son?

SOLO (Mary)

Just a few days from now, when I see this miracle, as I

hold His hand, will I understand what God has just begun? I know my God. The ways of God The ways of God

sometimes are hard to com-pre-hend

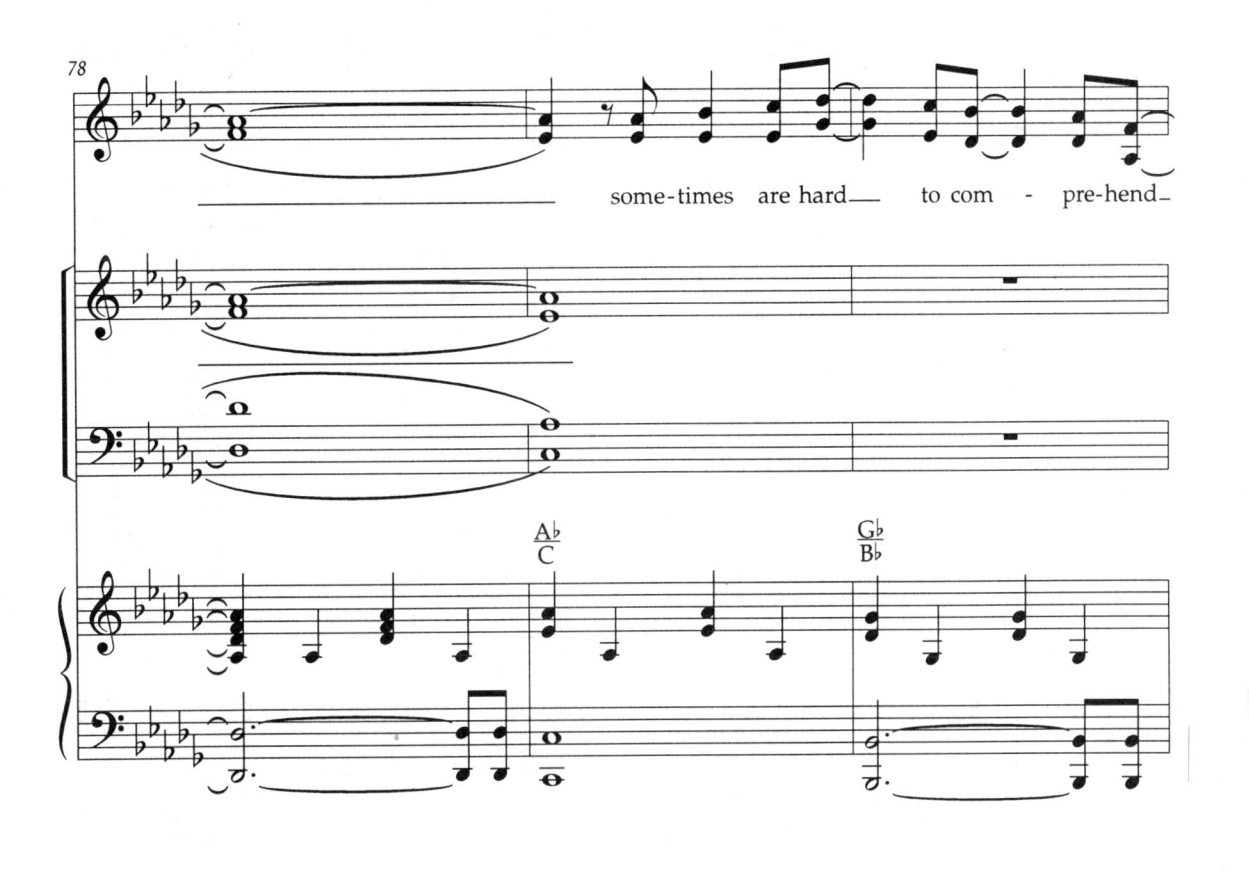

what's im-pos-si-ble for me is

Ah

pos - si - ble for Him. The ways of God

The ways of God

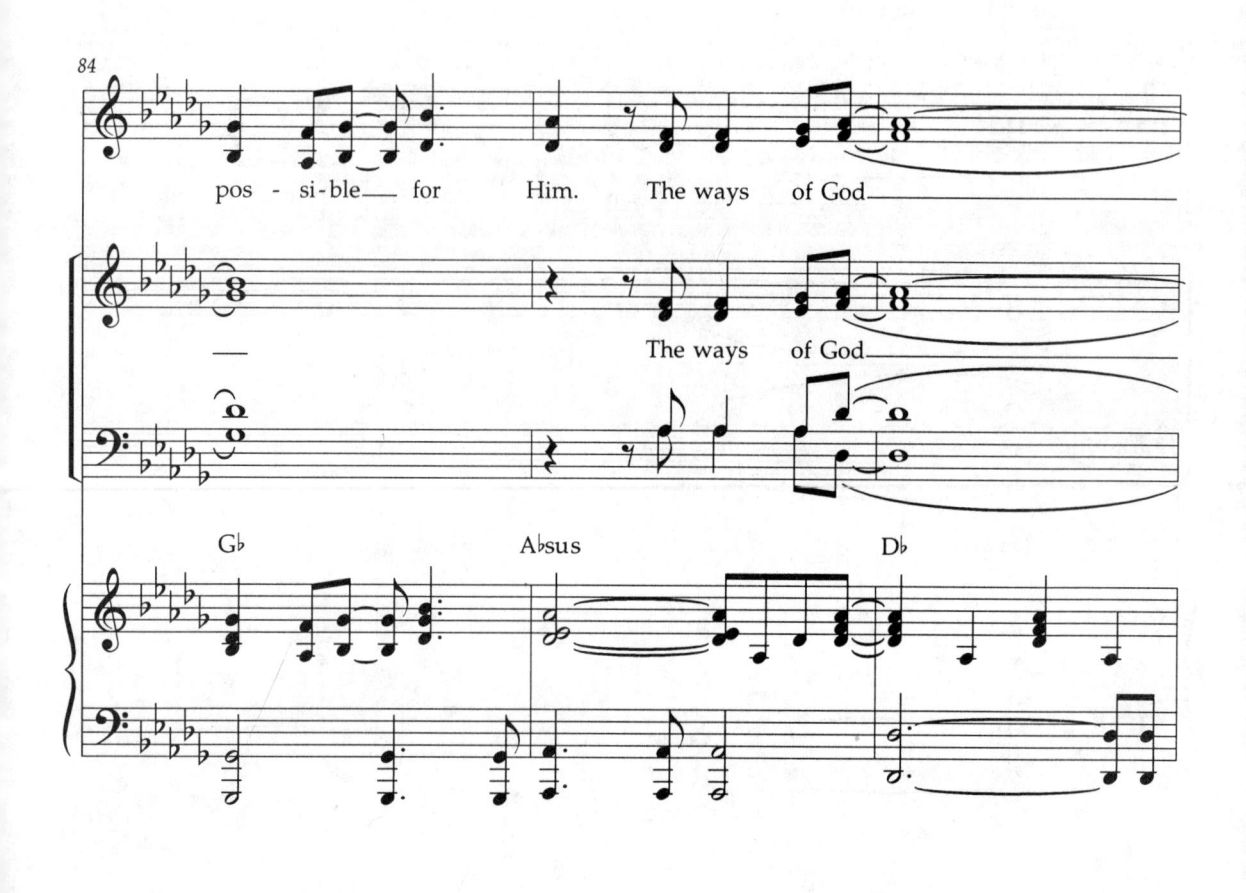

are so much high - er than my ways, like the

SOLO (Mary)

SOLO (Joseph)

heav - ens a - bove the earth, like the mir - a - cle of Je - sus' birth,

Ah

SOLO (Mary)

Still I will trust,

Still I will trust,

SOLO (Joseph)
96
still I will trust,
still I will trust,
Fm7 G♭maj7
E♭m7
Fm7
G♭maj7
99
DUET
still I will trust
still I will trust
Fm7 G♭maj7
E♭m7
A♭/D♭
G♭/C♭

41

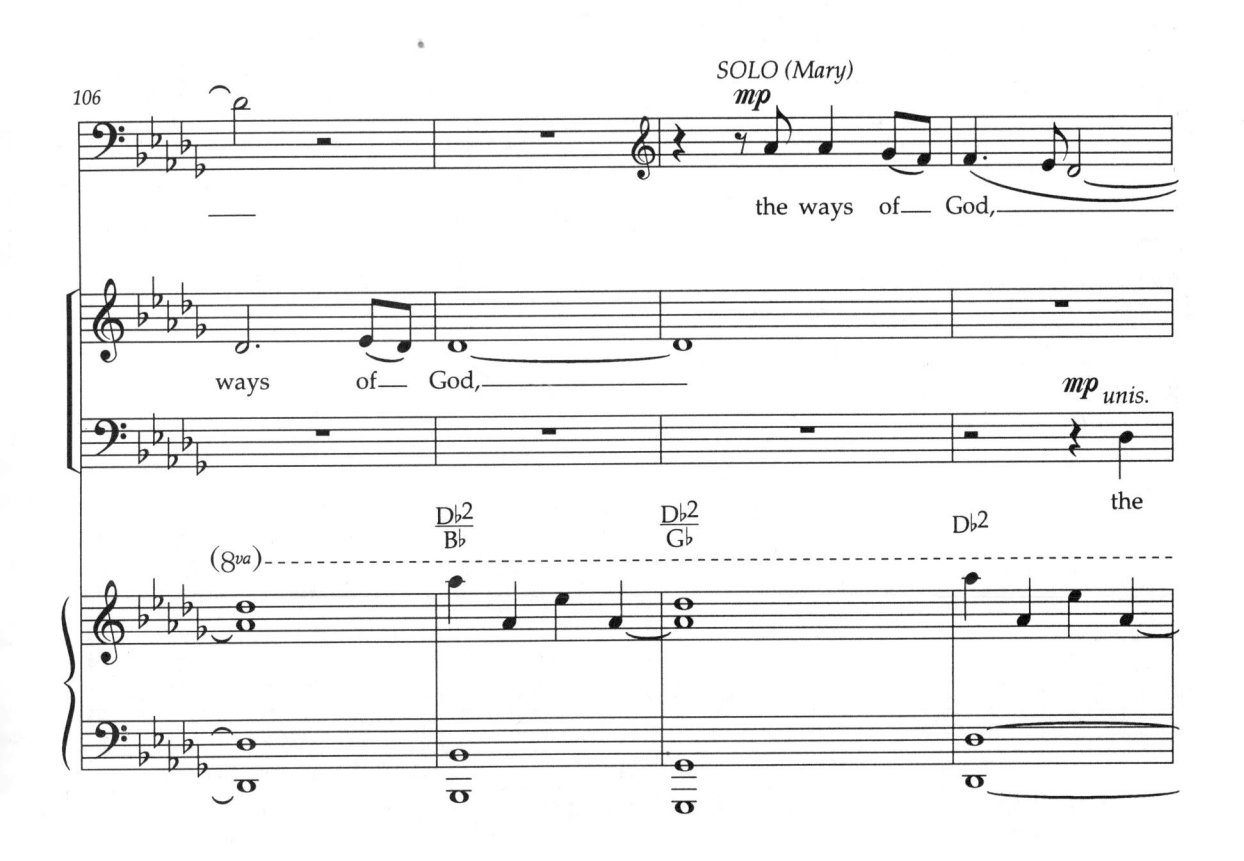

*These two bars may be used as a substitute ending if not using the narration or underscore found on page 43. Otherwise, ignore these two bars and segue directly to "When Hope Was Born."

When Hope Was Born
with
O Holy Night!

Words and Music by
CHRIS and DIANE MACHEN
Arranged by Camp Kirkland

NARRATION: So Joseph took Mary to Bethlehem, and while they were there, she gave birth to her firstborn Child. She wrapped Him in cloths and laid Him in a manger. On a cold winter's night, to a world without hope the gift of hope was born.

© Copyright 2001 Van Ness Press, Inc. (ASCAP).
Nashville, TN 37234.

When hope was born on a silent night, in the stillness lay the Child of Light. In a manger low, in a stable bare came the Prince of Peace to a world of care. Would they notice Him, would they bow before the Child of Light when hope was born?

When hope was born no fanfare played for an infant King in a

man - ger lay. But a star did shine on that humble place, for this Child would be God's work of grace. Not a king - ly throne, not a

pal - ace warm for the in - fant King when hope was born. When hope was born in Bethlehem, a Child would change the

hearts of men. For in God's great love for a world un-done He would sac-ri-fice His on-ly Son. And hope lives on like a fresh new morn in the hearts of men when hope was born.

More motion ♩. = 72

*O HOLY NIGHT**
More energy

thrill of hope, the weary world rejoices, for

*Words by John S. Dwight. Music by Adolphe Adam.
Arr. © Copyright 2001 Van Ness Press, Inc. (ASCAP). Nashville, TN 37234.

yon - der breaks a new and glo - rious morn.

Fall on your knees, O hear the an - gel voic - es. O

64
27 (2nd time)
unis.
night divine, O
unis.
D/A A/G D/F# G A/G G
66
div.
night when Christ was born. O
div.
D/A A/G D/F# Dsus/E D D/F#
68
1.
night di - vine, O
A A/G 1. D/A Gmaj9 Em/G

70
26
night, O night di-vine.
D/A A G/A A7 D A/C♯
72
2.
vine. O glo - rious
2. D/F♯ G2 G D/G Em/G
74
rit.
night, O night di - vine.
D/A A G/A A D
rit.

A little slower
mf
unis.
And hope lives on like a
unis.
A little slower
G
mf
fresh new morn in the hearts of men when
div.
rit.
div.
G/B
A/C♯
D
Bm
D/A
G
rit.
Segue to "Repeat the Sounding Joy"
hope was born.
Asus
A
D

Repeat the Sounding Joy

with
Joy to the World! The Lord Is Come

Words and Music by
CHRIS and DIANE MACHEN
and MIKE HARLAND
Arranged by Camp Kirkland

NARRATION: *(over music)* The Christ Child was born, and the joy that filled heaven spilled over to the earth. There were shepherds near Bethlehem keeping watch over their flocks of sheep that wondrous night. Suddenly, without warning, an angel appeared to them. They were terrified, but the angel said to them, "Don't be afraid. I have good news that will bring you great joy. Today, in Bethlehem, the Savior you've been waiting for has been born." And the world was given the gift of joy. Joy to the world! The Lord is come!

© Copyright 2001 Van Ness Press, Inc. (ASCAP).
Nashville, TN 37234.

shep-herds were watch-ing their flocks through the night when an an-gel ap-peared in the sky. "Don't be a-fraid, I have news of great joy," was the mes-sage he brought from on high. Then the heav - ens__ were filled with the heav - en - ly hosts for the joy was too great__ for one. And our shouts__ of praise still__ re-

-peat the refrain that the promised Messiah has come. Repeat the sounding joy, re-

33
peat the sound - ing joy,
our Sav - ior has come as a
B♭ F/A C B♭ F/A
36
30 (2nd time)
ba - by boy,
re - peat
1.
the sound - ing joy.
C♯dim7 Dm
1.
Gm7 F/A C7sus
38
Re -
2.
peat the sound - ing
unis.
C7
2.
Gm7 Csus C

*Words by Isaac Watts. Music by George Frederick Handel.
Arr. © Copyright 2001 Van Ness Press, Inc. (ASCAP). Nashville, TN 37234.

46
unis.
and heav-en and na - ture sing,
unis.
heav-en and na - ture sing,
and
D2
48
and heav-en and na - ture sing,
and
heav-en and na - ture sing,
Em
D
31
50
div.
heav'n and heav'n and na - ture sing.
div.
D
D
F♯
G
D
A
A♯dim7
Bm
G
D
A
A
D

52
Joy to the earth, the Sav - ior reigns, let
E♭ E♭/G A♭maj7 B♭ E♭
54
men their songs em - ploy. While
A♭ B♭ C♭ B♭m7 E♭
56
mf
fields and floods, rocks, hills and plains re -

58
peat the sound-ing joy,
re -
E♭
mf
32
60
peat the sound-ing joy,
re -
F
62
peat the sound-ing joy,
Re -
G

peat the sound-ing joy, re-peat the sound-ing joy, our Sav-ior has come as a ba-by boy, re-peat the sound-ing joy. Re-

A♭ | A♭/C | E♭ | D♭ | A♭/C | E♭ | D♭ | A♭/C

1. E dim7 | Fm | B♭m7 | A♭/C | E♭sus | E♭

72
2.
ba - by boy,
our Sav - ior has come,
2.
Edim7
Fm
B♭m7
Cm7
74
our Sav - ior has come,
C/E
Fm
Fm7
B♭m7
Cm7
76
re - peat
the
sound - ing
C/E
Fm
Fm7
B♭m7
E♭7sus
E♭7
D♭/E♭
E♭

79
joy,
re - peat the
A♭
A♭/D♭
B♭m7(4)
82
sound - ing
joy!
E♭7sus
E♭7
N.C.
A♭
F♭maj7
G♭
85
A♭

They Came to Worship
with
Angels, from the Realms of Glory

Words and Music by
CHRIS and DIANE MACHEN
Arranged by Camp Kirkland

NARRATION: *(music starts)* God, in His marvelous grace, gave. In His mercy, He gave a Savior. In His love, He gave the most precious gift of all—His Son, Jesus. How could we ever repay Him? What gift could we possibly give Him that would be worthy of the King of kings and Lord of lords? We can give Him our heart. We can give Him our life. And like the magi of old, we can give Him our worship.

© Copyright 2001 Van Ness Press, Inc. (ASCAP).
Nashville, TN 37234.

heav'n was clear and bright, the sky seemed lit by just a sin-gle star. And from a dis-tant land came a roy-al, re-gal band of stran-gers who had trav-eled from so far.

MEN unis. **mp** Pre-cious

gifts of price-less worth for the Sav-ior at His birth, the greatest King the world has ev-er known. And as they en-tered in, they bowed to wor-ship Him, and

1st time: Parts
2nd time: Unison, Stronger

laid their gifts be-fore His man-ger throne. They came to wor-ship Christ a - lone, they came to wor-ship at His throne. They brought their of - fer-ing for the new-born King who is wor-thy of all praise. They came to worship Christ a-lone, they came to worship at His throne. In the pres-ence of God's

71

an - gels came to praise Mes - si - ah's birth. Sal -

va - tion's mes - sage rang as the host of heav - en sang, the

Son of God would save the sons of earth. They came to

CODA
59
Stronger
unis.
name.
May the
unis.
CODA
E♭sus
E♭sus/B♭
E♭
3
61
praise they brought the in - fant King be the
E♭sus/B♭
E♭/B♭
Stronger
63
rit.
f
praise our hearts for - ev - er sing!
We've come to
E♭sus/B♭
Csus
C
Csus
C
rit.

worship Christ alone, we've come to worship at His throne. We bring our offering to the King of kings who is worthy of all praise, all

75
rit.
ff
praise.
We've come to
D♭/C♭
G♭/B♭ G♭sus/A♭ G♭ G♭/F♭
rit.
3
77
a tempo
div.
wor - ship Christ a - lone,
We've come to wor - ship at His
div.
G/D Gsus/A G Dsus D G G/B C B
ff a tempo
80
throne.
In the pres - ence of God's gift of love we give
Em Em/D C Am7 Bm7 Em D C Bm7

ANGELS, FROM THE REALMS OF GLORY*

*Words by James Montgomery. Music by Henry T. Smart.
Arr. © Copyright 2001 Van Ness Press, Inc. (ASCAP). Nashville, TN 37234.

wor - ship Christ, our Lord and King. He is Lord!

Worthy of My Lord

with
More Precious than Silver
O Come, All Ye Faithful

Words and Music by
CHRIS and DIANE MACHEN
and MIKE HARLAND
Arranged by Camp Kirkland

give You my heart, may it be as pure gold. I give You my praise as— in-cense of old. I give You my life as You gave me— Yours, may all that I bring be wor-thy of my Lord.

CHOIR
Wor-thy, wor-thy, wor-thy of my Lord, may all that I

bring be wor-thy of my Lord. I give You my
life as You gave me Yours. May all that I
bring be wor-thy of my Lord.

*MORE PRECIOUS THAN SILVER**
With Congregation

*Words and Music by Lynn DeShazo.
© Copyright 1982 and this arr. © 2001 Integrity's Hosanna! Music/ASCAP. c/o Integrity Incorporated,
1000 Cody Road, Mobile, AL 36695. All rights reserved. International copyright secured. Used by permission.

are more beau-ti-ful than dia-monds, and noth-ing I de-sire com-pares with You.

You. O

*O COME, ALL YE FAITHFUL**

come, all ye faith - ful, joy - ful and tri - um - phant, O come, ye, O come, ye to Beth - le - hem. Come and be -

*Words: Latin Hymn; ascribed to John Francis Wade; translated by Frederick Oakeley. Music by John Francis Wade.
Arr. © Copyright 2001 Van Ness Press, Inc. (ASCAP). Nashville, TN 37234.

70
hold Him born the King of an - gels. O
Fm7 Bb9 Eb Bb/D Eb Cm F/A Bb Cm/Bb Bb7 Ab/Bb
73
come, let us a - dore Him, O come, let us a -
Eb Bb/Eb Eb Fm/Eb Eb Bb/Eb Eb Ab/C
76
46
dore Him, O come, let us a - dore Him,
Eb/Bb Bb Eb Fm7 Eb Bb/D Cm Bb Bb/Ab Eb/G Ab/C

Christ the Lord. For He alone is worthy, for He alone is worthy, for He alone is worthy,

CHOIR only
mp
Christ the Lord. For He a - lone is
F/C C7sus C7 F Gm7 F C/E Dm
mp
rit.
wor - thy, Christ
C C/B♭ F/A B♭/D F/C
rit.
the Lord.
(7)
Csus C B♭/C F

# From the Cradle to the Cross

Mixed Trio, Ladies Trio, or Solo

Words and Music by
CHRIS and DIANE MACHEN
Arranged by Camp Kirkland

NARRATION: *(music starts)* As we bring Jesus the gift of our praise, we remember the wise men and their gifts—gifts worthy of a King. The gold represented deity, and the frankincense purity, but perhaps the most significant gift of all was the myrrh, for as a spice used in burial, it symbolized the very reason this King was born. He was born to die. This infant King who lay in a cradle would one day hang on a cross as our Savior, and all who believe in Him will receive God's greatest gift of love.

© Copyright 2001 Van Ness Press, Inc. (ASCAP).
Nashville, TN 37234.

Female SOLO **mf**

For God so loved the world— He gave His on-ly Son,— He was born in Beth-le-hem,— the work of grace be-gun.— In His sov-'reign, per-fect plan— He be-came like one of us,— to—

reach the heart of man— He gave Je - sus. From the

TRIO

CHOIR

From the

cra - dle to the cross,— from the Lord un - to the lost— came the

cra - dle to the cross,— from the Lord un - to the lost— came the mes-sage for all men,— Christ was born to die— for them. From

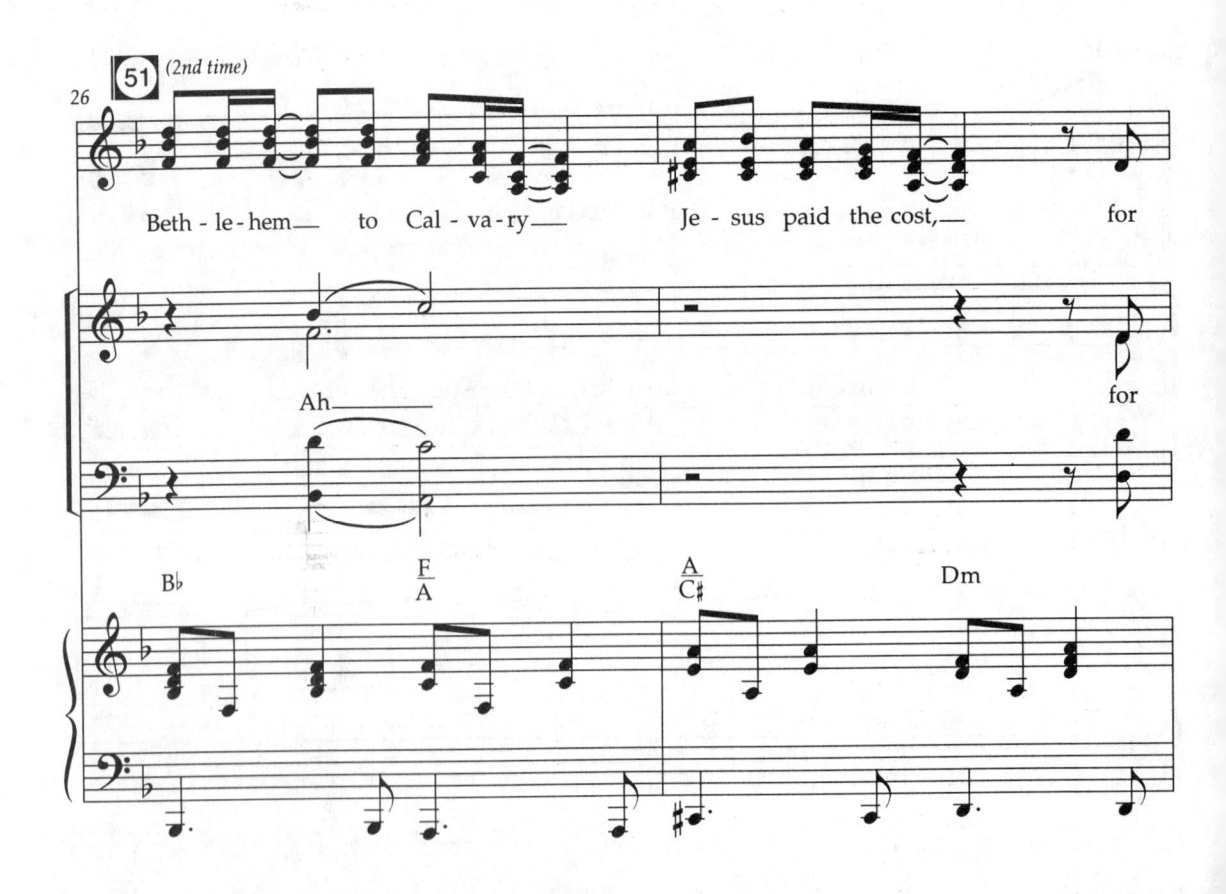

mes-sage for all men,— Christ was born to die— for them.

Beth-le-hem— to Cal-va-ry— Je-sus paid the cost,— for

Ah—

for

28
49 (1st time)
2nd time to Coda
love went all the way— from the cra - dle to the cross.
(CHOIR out)
love went all the way— from the cra - dle to the cross.
2nd time to Coda
F/C
Gm7
Gm/C
F
31
Male SOLO
mf
From the day—that He was born— the cross was call-ing—Him to the
E♭/B♭
B♭
F
C
mf
34
DUET
(add Female)
In a
place of sac - ri-fice— where grace would con - quer— sin. In a
B♭2
F/C
B♭/C
F/C
C
B♭/C

50
36
TRIO
man - ger Love was laid,
but Love was born to die,
at
man - ger Love was laid,
but Love was born to die,
at
F
C
D.S. al CODA
38
f
Cal - va - ry
Christ paid the high - est price!
From the
Cal - va - ry
Christ paid the high - est price!
D.S. al CODA
CHOIR
f
The high - est price! From the
D.S. al CODA
B♭
F/C
C
F/C
C
B♭/C

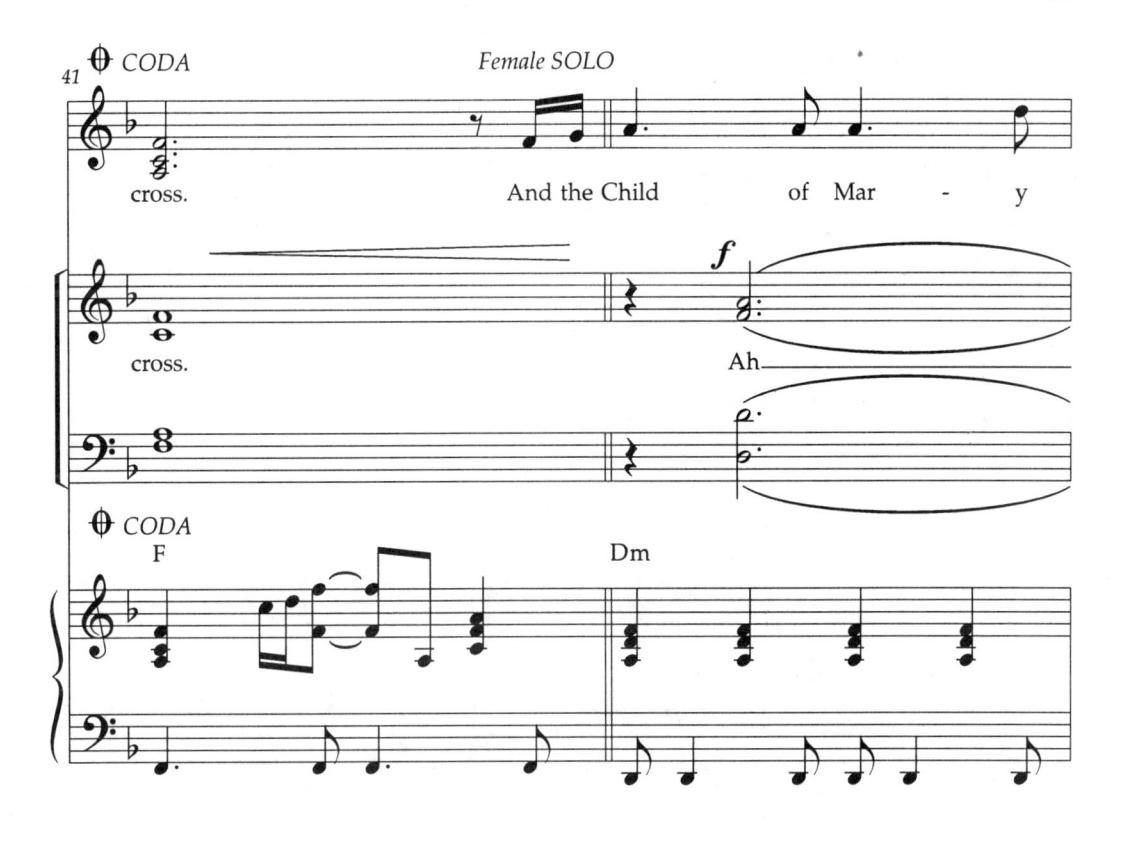

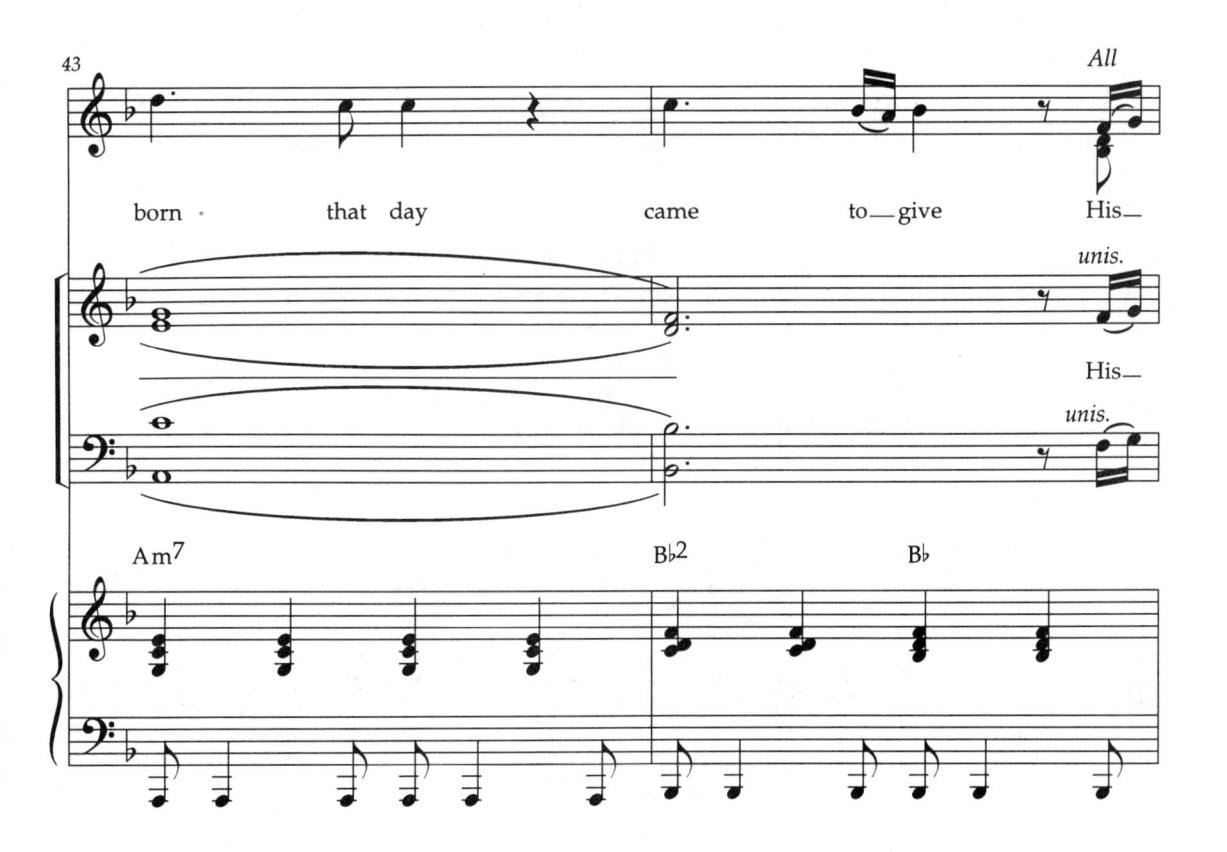

CODA   *Female SOLO*

cross.   And the Child of Mar - y

cross.   Ah___

CODA
F   Dm

born that day came to give His___ *All*

unis. His___

unis.

Am7   B♭2   B♭

life____ a - way, a - way!____

life____ a - way!____ *ff* From the

cra - dle to the cross,__ from the Lord un - to the lost,__ came the

ff came the

mes-sage for all men,— Christ was born to die— for them. From

mes-sage for all men,— Christ was born to die— for them.

Beth-le-hem— to Cal-va-ry— Je-sus paid the cost,— for

Ah— for

52
53
love went all the way from the cra - dle to the
love went all the way from the cra - dle to the
G/D
Am7
Am/D
Am7/D

55
cross. From Beth - le - hem to Cal - va - ry Je - sus paid the
ff
cross. Ah Je - sus paid the
G
C
G/B
B/D♯

58
Female SOLO
cost,
Yes,
cost,
for Love went all the way,
Em
G
D
60
Male SOLO
Love went all the way,
yes,
Love went all the way,
Em

62
Female SOLO
Love went all the way,
yes,
Love went all the way
Am7
64
TRIO
Love went all the way
from the cra - dle
from the cra - dle
G
B

66
3
to the cross, to the cross,
to the cross, to the
C D G F2 F C C/D

69
big rit.
to the cross, to the cross!
big rit.
cross, to the cross!
G F C C/D G
8va
big rit.

Gift of Heaven (Finale)

includes
Gift of Heaven
For a Child Will Be Born
Repeat the Sounding Joy

Words and Music by
CHRIS and DIANE MACHEN
Arranged by Camp Kirkland

NARRATION: *(music starts)* For God so loved the world that He gave: He gave light to those in darkness; He gave hope to those without hope; He gave life and joy and love; He gave Jesus, the gift of heaven. Thanks be to God for His indescribable gift!

© Copyright 2001 Van Ness Press, Inc. (ASCAP).
Nashville, TN 37234.

101

dark - ened world— He is light, to a dy - ing heart— He is life. To a wound - ed soul— He is the Heal - er, Je - sus, Je - sus.

D.S. al CODA

en.

To a troubled life___ He is peace, to a captive heart,___ liberty. To a world in sin___ He is forgiveness,

57
38
Je - sus, Je - sus.
Bbm7 Ab/C Db Ebsus Eb
41
f unis.
Je - sus, gift of heav - en, Je - sus,
unis.
Ab Bbm7 Cm7 Eb/F Ab/Eb Db Ab/C
f
44
div.
pre-cious gift of love from the heart of God to the
div.
Bbm7 Ebsus Eb Fm Eb/G Ab

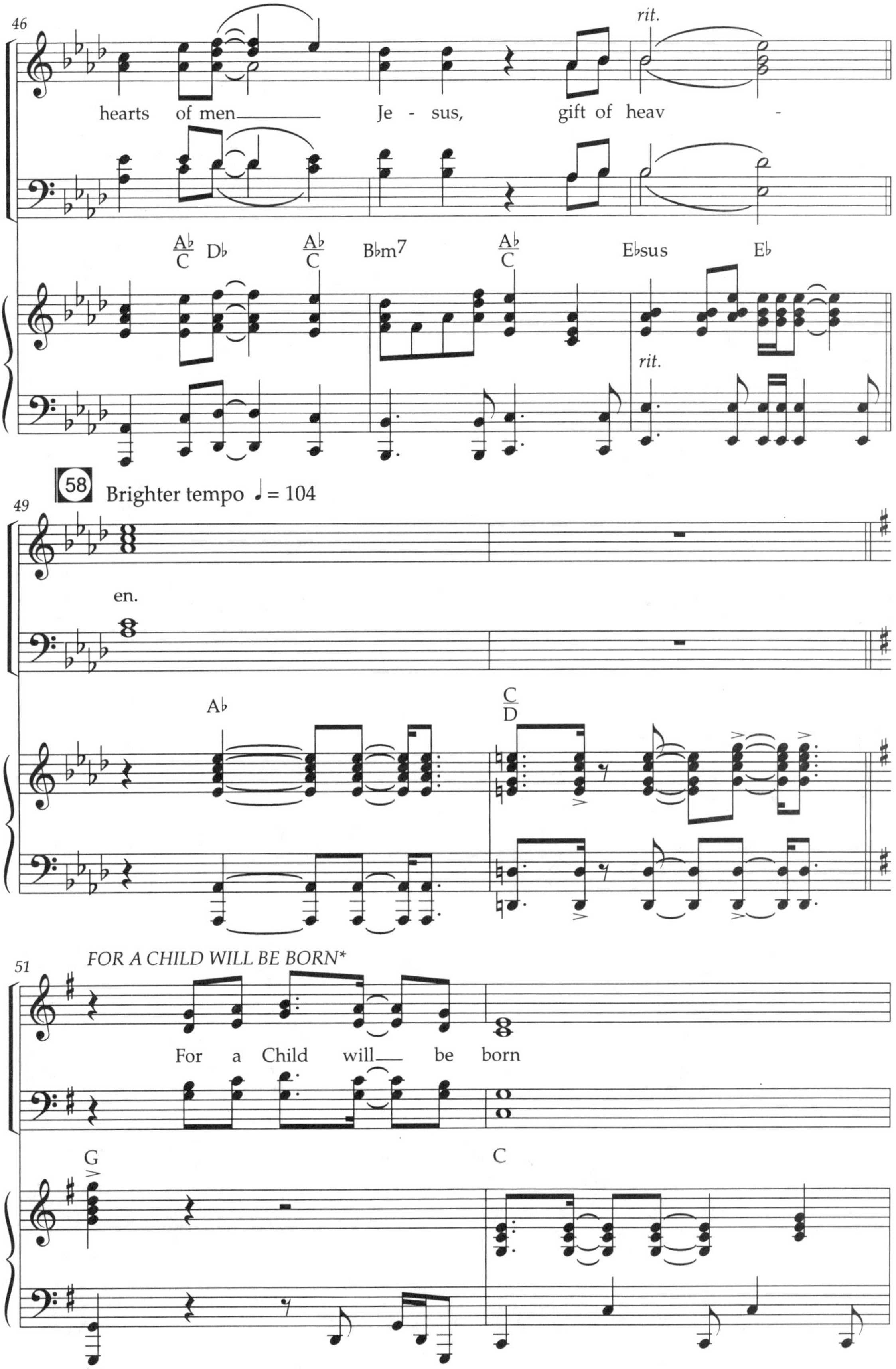

and a Son will be giv - en, for a Child will be born and a Son will be giv - en.

be born

And His name shall be called Wonderful

Ev-er-last-ing Fa-ther, the Coun-se-lor, Might-y God, Prince of Peace, the Light will come.

For a Child will be

70
div.
born,
and a Son will — be giv - en. —
div.
For a Child will — be born,
giv - en. —
D♭
E♭
E♭/A♭
A♭
73
unis.
For a Child will — be born, —
unis.
For a Child will be born, —
B♭m/A♭
A♭
B♭m/A♭
A♭
D♭
E♭/D♭
D♭maj7
E♭
75
div.
and a Son will — be giv - en. —
The Light has
div.
— giv - en. —
E♭/A♭
A♭
A♭/C

109

*Words and Music by Chris and Diane Machen and Mike Harland.
© Copyright 2001 Van Ness Press, Inc. (ASCAP). Nashville, TN 37234.

peat the sound-ing joy, repeat the sound-ing joy, our Sav-ior has come as a ba-by boy, re- peat the sound-ing joy. Repeat the sound-ing joy, repeat the sound-ing joy,

our Sav-ior has come as a ba-by boy, our Sav-ior has come, our

Sav-ior has come,— re-peat the sound-ing joy,— re-peat the sound-ing joy!

Je - sus, gift of heav - en, Je - sus, pre - cious gift of love. From the heart of God to the

118
hearts of men, Je - sus, gift of heav -
B♭/D E♭ B♭/D Cm7 B♭/D Fsus F
121
en. Je - sus, gift of
B♭ B♭sus/C B♭/D B♭sus/C B♭ B♭/D Cm7 B♭/D
A little faster ♩ = 104
123
rit.
heav - en. He is
A little faster ♩ = 104
Fsus F B♭
rit.

love, He is light, He is hope, He is joy, He is Je - sus. He is the gift of heav - en!

GIFT of HEAVEN

Production Notes
by Lisa C. Parker

Gift of Heaven can be divided into two parts:
- Part I retells the Christmas story simply and beautifully, while
- Part II leads the congregation into a time of personal reflection on their relationship with Jesus. The open format (a simple set up consisting of a narrator between songs) offers multiple options for presentation, from doing the work "as-is" with no extras, to adding as much drama, props, set, and lighting as you can use in your facility!

The suggestions offered here are for dramatic presentation using simple props and characters in biblical dress. Lighting is limited to dimmable house lights and one or two spotlights; however, there are many places for churches having more choices to creatively use what they have.

Overture / Processional

House lights fade to black (possibly during prayer before the music starts). A spot comes up at center stage: Isaiah walks into the spot holding a scroll and dressed in biblical costume (or use the narrator). During measures 1-17 of the Overture he sets up the opening number by reading from the scroll with a strong voice:

This is the message the Lord has given to Isaiah the prophet: "Behold, a virgin shall conceive, and bear a son, and shall call his name Immanuel…unto us a child is born, unto us a son is given: and the government shall be upon his shoulder: and his name shall be called Wonderful, Counselor, The mighty God, The everlasting Father, The Prince of Peace" (Isa. 7:14; 9:6).

At measure 19 the choir can enter either from the back of the auditorium or from their normal entrances and quietly take their places. Encourage them to enter with smiles and an attitude of expectation—they just can't wait to see what the Lord is going to do here!

"Gift of Heaven" (Opening)

If you used the Overture, have the stage-area lights slowly fade up during the last two measures of the Overture and the introduction. The lights should be full up just before the choir begins to sing.

This number stands alone as a great anthem for Advent Sundays, and you can also use measure 20 to the end of the song (skipping the first verse) as a call to worship.

"House of Bread"

It is well known that we retain more with visuals than with any other means of information transfer. For this number, the lyric strongly supports the use of slides or still shots projected onto a large screen of small villages and people in the holy land during Bible times. You may also wish to include pictures of bread used during Jewish holidays, bread at the Last Supper, etc. If possible, coordinating pictures with the lyric will bring about the best effect. Combined with the song, the desired connection between the "house of bread," the Bread of life, and the promise that we will never hunger or thirst again will be well made.

"The Ways of God"

Leave the stage-area lights down after "House of Bread" and bring a spot up on Mary, who enters during the narration (cue—"a young maiden named Mary"). At almost the same time, Joseph enters a spot from the opposite side of the stage. Both are dressed in biblical costume (including a head covering for Mary). Joseph kneels as if praying while Mary sings her solo. He then stands to sing his part. They sing the first verse and chorus at opposite sides of the platform, not looking at each other. The soloists should put enough expression in their voices and bodies to make the congregation think about what Mary and Joseph must have felt.

As Joseph begins the second verse, both characters can move closer to center stage. At the second chorus, as they both stand at center, they should look at each other, and on the final chorus, Mary and Joseph look out over the congregation, emphasizing the truth of this message.

"When Hope Was Born"

As narration begins, Joseph takes Mary's hand and they go offstage slowly. Lights go to black and a manger filled with hay is placed center stage in the dark.

A spot comes up on the manger during the first verse of the song, and as the men begin to sing the second verse, Mary and Joseph return carrying a baby (yes, a real one) wrapped in a white cotton blanket. In case of a crying spell, station the real mother just offstage dressed in biblical costume. If the baby cries, first have Mary or Joseph hand the baby to the other, and change its position. If crying persists, have the real mother come onstage and take the baby off. Most of the time the babies do just fine, and there's nothing more moving than seeing those tiny arms and feet moving and thinking about the God of the universe taking on this small form! It is important to rehearse this with everyone involved.

The stage-area lights can slowly fade up to full during "O Holy Night," fading back down during the quiet tag at the end of the song.

You may wish to have older children or youth dressed in white robes (angels) enter carrying lit candles during "O Holy Night" and kneel the second time the choir sings, "fall on your knees." (NOTE: Votive candles placed inside glass cup-shaped holders work well and are inexpensive. You may also want to check out battery-powered candles. They cost more to purchase, but are very safe and can be used many times over.) On the final phrase of the song, the angels lift their candles high and freeze in position.

"Repeat the Sounding Joy"

As the narration begins, candles are extinguished and the angels move to either side of the stage area. Be sure to place them in different postures (standing, kneeling, sitting, etc.) to add visual interest and avoid blocking sight lines.

As the choir begins singing, a spotlight picks up several shepherds positioned on one side of the stage area as if out in the fields. Their pantomimed actions should work with the song lyric, and they come to the stage area quickly, showing fear and confusion. When they arrive, their fear gives way to joy! One or two might bow in worship, while Mary hands the baby to another. Make this as "human" and real as possible. Let them move, interacting with Mary, Joseph, and the baby. Only the angels are static, looking on in worship.

The stage area lights have come up full at the shepherds' arrival, and at measure 40, consider using a procession of "Joy" banners! Make them of different sizes, shapes and fabrics, but each should be brightly colored and the word "Joy" may appear on several or all of them. Include lots of donated materials: sequins, old costume jewelry, ribbon streamers, beads, and bells! They can process from the back to positions all over the auditorium, as well as the platform, steps, even behind the choir, as room allows.

Make sure they have plenty of help getting in to clear overhead structures, and know where to enter and exit. (Labeled gaffers' tape on the floor works well.)

Time the entrance of the banners so that the last few are in place by measure 80.

At the end of this song, you have the holy family, shepherds, angels, and banners everywhere—a "joyful" scene indeed!

After the cut-off, stage area lights go to black, and all characters and banners exit.

"They Came to Worship"

During the narration, a single spot comes up on the empty hay-filled manger and the stage/choir lights come up slowly when the choir begins singing.

The Magi enter from the back of the auditorium with their gifts which they lay at the manger one at a time before bowing low on one side of the stage. At measure 49, several angels enter and take places opposite the Magi. (You may want these angels to look slightly different than the earlier ones.) Once all are in place, they, too, bow low before the manger.

At measure 60, have several people representing our world today come forward singly or in small groups: a doctor, business person, policeman, day-care worker, people from other nations, a family, etc.

Using modern day people is a visual symbol of the transition *Gift of Heaven* makes here from Part I (watching a story) to Part II (becoming a part of that story)! Now we are invited to apply the truths we've seen to our lives and open our hearts to Him in worship.

Modern day people spread out across the floor in front of the stage from side to side facing the manger. At measure 88, the Magi raise their hands up and toward center stage in praise to God, and at measure 90, the angels do the same. At measure 92 the people of the world kneel, and at measure 96, they raise their hands upward toward the manger. Everyone holds this position until the song is over.

The stage area lights fade to black and all characters exit, leaving the manger at center stage. (Make sure the Magi gifts are removed.)

"Worthy of My Lord"

This should be a time of personal praise. Spot the soloist, and have the stage/choir lights fade up at measure 41 as the worship leader or soloist invites the congregation to sing along. You may wish to print the words in the program or project them for the congregation to follow.

"From the Cradle to the Cross"

This song presents the main point of the message. As the male solo begins at measure 31, a "cross" banner can be brought down the aisle and placed at center stage right behind the manger—a strong visual connection of the cradle to the cross. Around measure 65, bring the stage area lights down to a spot illuminating only the manger and the cross. (Solos and trio can be placed at either side of center stage.)

This would be a good time for your pastor to offer an invitation and prayer!

"Gift of Heaven" (Finale)

This is a great closer—an "Amen" to the service. It really doesn't call for any visuals; however, you can bring back all characters seen during the evening and place them across the stage area and floor. For example, at measure 51, Isaiah and all angels enter; at measure 68, the shepherds and Magi. At measure 85, the "Joy" banners take places and at measure 113, the modern day people. Finally, at measure 122, Mary, Joseph, and the baby take places at center stage in front of the cross banner and next to the manger.

This is a nice big finish to go along with the nice big ending of the music! However, make it clear that this is not a "curtain call." All the glory belongs to Jesus!

Additional Uses

You can easily use *Gift of Heaven* in a variety of ways throughout the Christmas season and beyond!

• If you wish to present a shorter service, start with the Overture, followed by "House of Bread," then "The Ways of God," including all narration and underscoring. Combine the narration for "When Hope Was Born" with the narration for "Repeat the Sounding Joy" followed by that song. End with "They Came to Worship." You've presented the story, and challenged the congregation to come and worship!

• "Worthy of My Lord" is an excellent choir anthem. Or, as part of your song service, have the choir sing up to measure 43. Then, invite the congregation to join you for the rest of the song. What a beautiful worship medley!

• For a "stand alone" choir-only special, look at "From the Cradle to the Cross." This powerful theme, centered on the cross, is structured around solos and a trio. In addition, this anthem can be done any time of the year, and especially around Easter.

• "When Hope Was Born" makes a very effective Christmas season choir special.

I hope these suggestions provide a springboard of ideas to help you organize and carry out a musical worship experience that will draw you, your choir, and your congregation closer to the Lord Jesus!

Lisa C. Parker serves as the Preteen Choir Supervisor at Bellevue Baptist Church in the Memphis, Tennessee, area. Additionally, she has written scripts for a number of the outstanding seasonal productions at Bellevue and sings in the Sanctuary Choir under the direction of Dr. Jim Whitmire.